AF207153

Leonardo da Vinci (1452-1519) was born in Italy, the son of a gentleman of Florence. He made significant contributions to many different disciplines, including anatomy, botany, geology, astronomy, architecture, paleontology, and cartography.

He is one of the greatest and most influential painters of all time, creating masterpieces such as the *Mona Lisa* and *The Last Supper*. And his imagination led him to create designs for things such as an armored car, scuba gear, a parachute, a revolving bridge, and flying machines. Many of these ideas were so far ahead of their time that they weren't built until centuries later.

He is the original "Renaissance Man" whose genius extended to all five areas of today's STEAM curriculum: Science, Technology, Engineering, the Arts, and Mathematics.

You can find more information on Leonardo da Vinci in *Who Was Leonardo da Vinci?* by Roberta Edwards (Grosset & Dunlap, 2005), *Magic Tree House Fact Tracker: Leonardo da Vinci* by Mary Pope Osborne and Natalie Pope Bryce (Random House, 2009), and *Leonardo da Vinci for Kids: His Life and Ideas* by Janis Herbert (Chicago Review Press, 1998).

Fascinating World
of TECHNOLOGY

Illustrated by
GREG PAPROCKI

Written by
BOB COOPER

GIBBS SMITH
TO ENRICH AND INSPIRE HUMANKIND

TECHNOLOGY comes from using our understanding of science, engineering, mathematics, and the arts to INVENT and build things that are useful and make our lives easier.

Throughout history, inventions have improved how things are done, and sometimes performed tasks that have never even been thought of before.

Important inventions that have dramatically changed our way of life include the PRINTING PRESS, ELECTRIC LIGHTS, the TELEPHONE, and TV.

Since the last half of the twentieth century, new technology has been introduced at a faster and faster rate.

The SPACE PROGRAM of the 1960s and '70s was an important reason for this technology boom.

In addition to landing astronauts on the Moon, it resulted in thousands of innovations in medicine, transportation, computers, cameras, fabrics, food science, waste disposal, and many other things.

Ever since the invention of the WHEEL, inventing new and better VEHICLES for getting from one place to another more quickly has been an important area of technology.

It used to be quite an adventure just getting from the farm to town. Horse-drawn carts eventually led to faster and faster AUTOMOBILES.

AIRPLANES allowed travel across continents and oceans in just a few hours. And now we're developing SPACECRAFT to fly from the Earth to Mars!

Just like we rely on networks of roads and highways for a fast and easy means of transportation, we also rely on large POWER TRANSMISSION SYSTEMS to provide electricity to our homes and businesses.

The power for these systems is generated by things like coal, natural gas, the wind, and the sun.

Technology that uses RENEWABLE ENERGY sources, like SOLAR PANELS that convert the sun's rays into power and WIND TURBINES that capture the power of the wind, makes our energy use cleaner and more efficient.

Technology has helped us build a vast communications network so that we can instantly communicate with people around the world.

Hundreds of SATELLITES orbiting the Earth are an important part of this network.

ELECTRONIC DEVICES like phones and computers
have become increasingly smaller, faster, and more powerful.

The COMPUTERS that guided astronauts to
the moon in the 1960s had less computing power than
the microwave oven that's in your kitchen today.

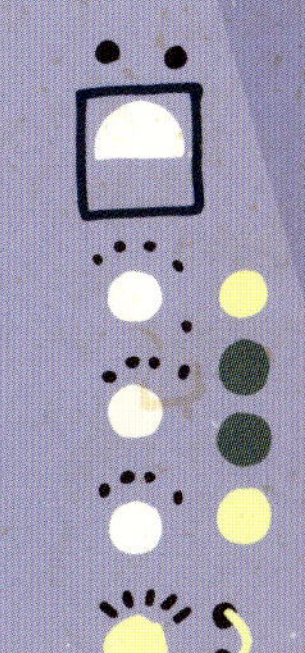

Today we carry around SMARTPHONES in our pockets
that are 100 million times faster than a 1960s supercomputer.

In addition to smartphones, we now have smart wristwatches, eyeglasses, and other WEARABLE TECHNOLOGY. Are smart tattoos that monitor your health the next technological innovation?

A lot of current innovation is with the SOFTWARE that runs on computers and other electronic devices.
CODERS write software using PROGRAMMING LANGUAGES. Different kinds of programming languages are used for things like creating games and APPS, and organizing data in DATABASES.

Machines called ROBOTS, controlled by simple computer code, now do some of the physical manufacturing jobs that humans used to do.

There are more INDUSTRIAL ROBOTS than humans on some of today's automobile assembly lines.

Machines with ARTIFICIAL INTELLIGENCE can make decisions and solve problems more quickly than we can.
There are artificial intelligences that can play (and win!) games of chess. And some are being developed that can even drive cars.

CO-BOTS (collaborative robots) are programmed to work alongside humans to help us do our jobs.
Using artificial intelligence, they can learn how to do something by watching *us* do it and then copying what we do.

Humans can quickly react to changes and new things, and can often come up with brand new solutions to problems. But we can't process data as quickly or move as carefully and precisely as co-bots can.

Together, humans and co-bots can make a great team.

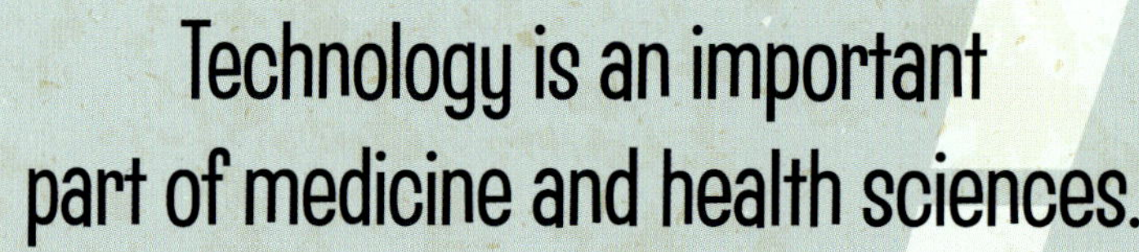

Technology is an important
part of medicine and health sciences.

Surgical co-bots are more precise than human surgeons,
allow faster healing, and create smaller scars.

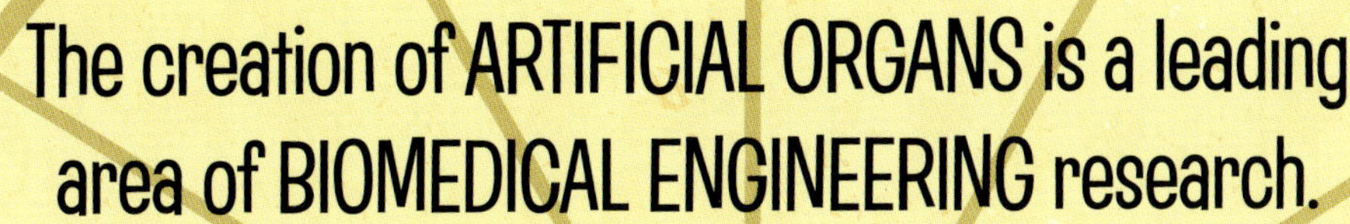

The creation of ARTIFICIAL ORGANS is a leading area of BIOMEDICAL ENGINEERING research.

Artificial hearts are used to keep patients alive while they wait for a heart transplant. Artificial kidneys are being developed to replace large and expensive dialysis machines.

Technology today is everywhere.
1000
It lets us keep in touch with each other, moves us from place to place, entertains us, feeds us, keeps us healthy, and does a lot of other things for us.

What kind of technology are *you* most interested in?

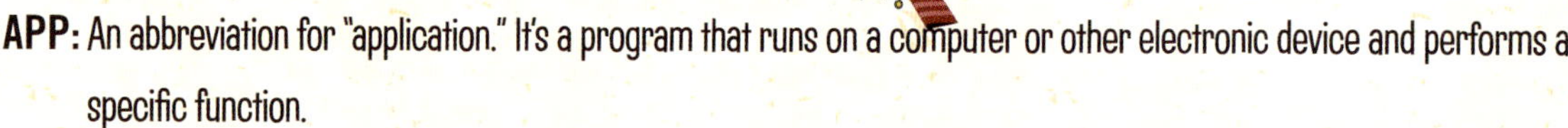

GLOSSARY

AIRPLANE: A vehicle with wings that travels through the air.

APP: An abbreviation for "application." It's a program that runs on a computer or other electronic device and performs a specific function.

ARTIFICIAL INTELLIGENCE: (art-uh-fish-ull in-TELL-uh-jintz): A machine that can learn and act with what appears to be human intelligence and reason.

ARTIFICIAL ORGAN: (art-uh-fish-ull OR-gun): A machine or device used to replace an actual organ in the body, such as an artificial lung.

AUTOMOBILE: (ott-uh-moe-BEAL): A vehicle designed to carry people and travel on roads and highways.

BIOMEDICAL ENGINEERING: (by-oh-med-ick-ull en-juh-NEAR-ing): An area of engineering that uses knowledge of biology and medicine to help with medical diagnoses and treatment, including creating devices such as prosthetic limbs and artificial organs.

CO-BOT (CO-bot): An abbreviation for "collaborative robot." A robot that works alongside humans to help them perform tasks.

CODER (CO-dur): Someone who writes computer programs using a programming language.

COMPUTER: An electronic machine that stores and works with large amounts of information.

DATABASE (DAY-tuh-base): An organized collection of information stored on a computer.

ELECTRIC LIGHT: (uh-LECK-trick light): A device that produces artificial light using electricity.

ELECTRONIC DEVICE: (uh-leck-TRON-ick duh-VICE): Any device that runs on electricity; especially referring to small programmable devices like laptop computers, tablets, cameras, and cell phones.

INDUSTRIAL ROBOT (in-dus-tree-ul ROW-bot): A robot used to perform physical manufacturing tasks, like assembly, welding, painting, and packaging.

INVENT: To be the first to create or produce something new and useful.

POWER TRANSMISSION SYSTEM (pow-ur trans-MISH-un sis-tum): A system for moving electricity from a power plant along a network of wires to homes and businesses.

PRINTING PRESS: A machine that prints pages for books, magazines, newspapers, and other reading materials.

PROGRAMMING LANGUAGE (PRO-gram-ing lang-gwudge): A language used to create programs and applications that run on computers and other electronic devices. 

RENEWABLE ENERGY (re-NEW-uh-bull EN-urr-gee): Energy that comes from natural resources such as the sun, wind, and water that naturally replenish themselves.

ROBOT: A machine that does the work of a person, either automatically or controlled by a computer.

SATELLITE (SAT-uh-light): A spacecraft permanently orbiting the Earth that is used for communication, weather monitoring, and other things. 

SMARTPHONE: A cell phone that includes many more functions than a regular telephone, including such things as e-mail, calendar, Internet, camera, and navigation apps.

SOFTWARE: Programs that run on a computer or other electronic device and perform specific functions.

SOLAR PANEL (SO-lur pan-ul): A flat piece of material that absorbs the sun's rays and converts them to heat or electricity.

SPACE PROGRAM: A planned series of explorations into space; most famously, America's series of space flights in the 1960s and early 1970s that led to landing men on the moon. 

SPACECRAFT: A vehicle that travels in space. 

TECHNOLOGY (teck-NALL-uh-gee): The application of science, math, engineering, and the arts to solve problems and invent new and useful things.

TELEPHONE (TELL-uh-fone): A device used to listen and speak to someone else at another location.

TV: An abbreviation for TELEVISION. An electronic device that broadcasts sounds and images, primarily for entertainment, either wirelessly or along a network of wires and cables.

VEHICLE (VEE-uh-cull): A machine that moves and is used to transport people or things from one place to another.

WEARABLE TECHNOLOGY (WHERE-uh-bull teck-NALL-uh-gee): Electronic devices that are worn on the body, like smart wristwatches. 

WHEEL: A circular object that rotates; used on vehicles and other mechanical devices to allow them to move. One of the very first important inventions.

WIND TURBINE (WIND tur-bin): A tall structure with rotating blades used to produce electricity.

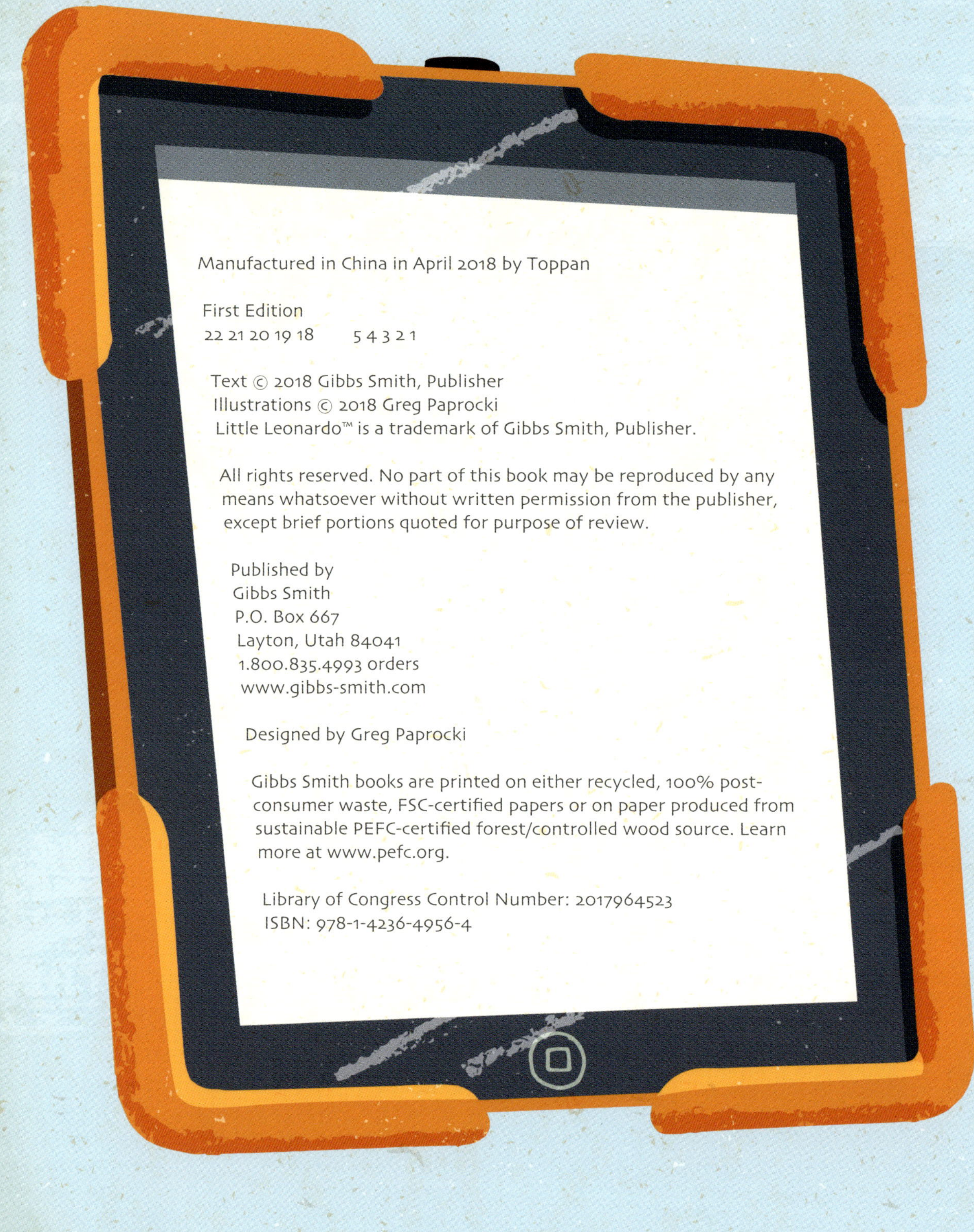

Manufactured in China in April 2018 by Toppan

First Edition
22 21 20 19 18   5 4 3 2 1

Text © 2018 Gibbs Smith, Publisher
Illustrations © 2018 Greg Paprocki
Little Leonardo™ is a trademark of Gibbs Smith, Publisher.

All rights reserved. No part of this book may be reproduced by any means whatsoever without written permission from the publisher, except brief portions quoted for purpose of review.

Published by
Gibbs Smith
P.O. Box 667
Layton, Utah 84041
1.800.835.4993 orders
www.gibbs-smith.com

Designed by Greg Paprocki

Gibbs Smith books are printed on either recycled, 100% post-consumer waste, FSC-certified papers or on paper produced from sustainable PEFC-certified forest/controlled wood source. Learn more at www.pefc.org.

Library of Congress Control Number: 2017964523
ISBN: 978-1-4236-4956-4

Some significant inventors . . .

Sybilla Righton Masters (ca. 1676–1720)

She was the first person from the American colonies to be given an English patent, and may have been the first American woman inventor. In 1715 she was granted a patent for a new method of creating cornmeal from corn, which used a stamping process instead of grinding and was powered by a horse or waterwheel.

Elijah McCoy (1844–1929)

The son of slaves who had escaped to Canada via the Underground Railroad, he traveled by himself as a teenager to Scotland, where he earned a mechanical engineering degree. He patented his first invention in 1872, and eventually held a total of 57 patents, including for a lawn sprinkler and an ironing board. One of his most important inventions was a lubrication device that distributed oil evenly over a train engine's moving parts.

Thomas Edison (1847–1931)

Known as the "Wizard of Menlo Park," he was one of the most important inventors in American history. Among his more important inventions were the first practical incandescent light bulb, the phonograph, alkaline batteries, an improved two-way telegraph system, and a camera for filming motion pictures.

Stephanie Kwolek (1923–2014)

She was an American chemist best known for inventing Kevlar, an extremely strong and lightweight synthetic fiber now used in everything from bulletproof vests to retractable roofs on sports stadiums. She won a number of awards for her work in polymer chemistry, and in 1995 became the fourth woman to be inducted into the National Inventors Hall of Fame.

Walt Braithwaite (1945–)

He joined Boeing as an engineer in 1966. In the 1970s, he helped develop the first computer-aided design/computer-aided manufacturing (CAD/CAM) systems to help in the design of commercial airplanes. He helped supervise the engineering development of Boeing's commercial airplanes through the 1990s, and became the highest-ranking black executive at Boeing when he was named president of Boeing Africa in 2000.

Ann Makosinski (1997–)

She began inventing things when she was seven years old. When she was 15 she invented a flashlight made from a special material that produces light when one side is heated and the other side remains cool, so that nothing more than the warmth of someone's hand holding the flashlight produces a steady beam of light. There will likely be many more ideas from her still to come . . .

TECHNOLOGY